Vocal Selections from the Motion Picture

Applications for performance of this work, whether legitimate, stock,
amateur, or foreign, should be addressed to:
MUSIC THEATRE INTERNATIONAL
545 Eighth Avenue
New York, NY 10018

Annie
T.M.

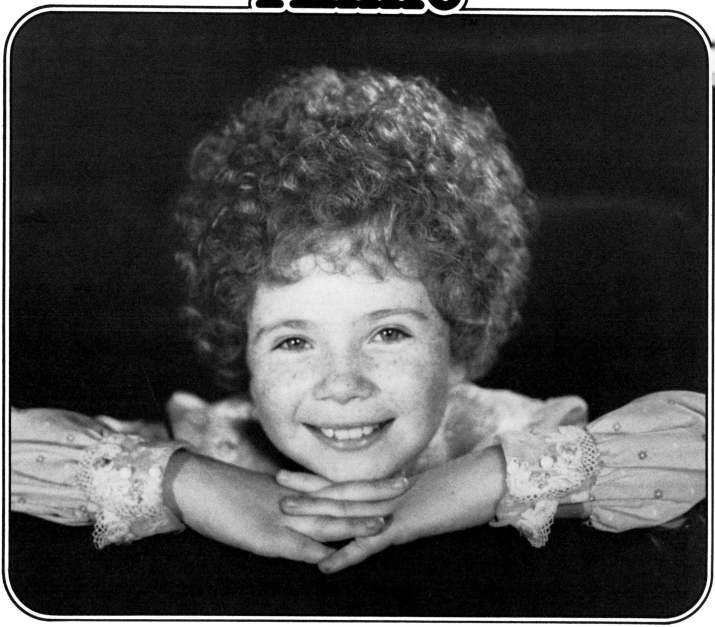

49 EASY STREET
39 I DON'T NEED ANYTHING BUT YOU
20 I THINK I'M GONNA LIKE IT HERE
12 IT'S THE HARD-KNOCK LIFE
28 LET'S GO TO THE MOVIES
46 LITTLE GIRLS
7 MAYBE
24 SANDY (DUMB DOG)
32 SIGN!
10 TOMORROW
17 WE GOT ANNIE
43 YOU'RE NEVER FULLY DRESSED WITHOUT A SMILE

MAYBE

Lyric by MARTIN CHARNIN
Music by CHARLES STROUSE

TOMORROW

Lyric by Martin Charnin
Music by Charles Strouse

The sun'll come out___ to-mor-row, bet your bot-tom dol-lar that to- mor-row___ there'll be sun! Just

think-ing a-bout___ to-mor-row clears a-way the cob-webs and the sor-row___ 'til there's none. When I'm stuck with a

day that's gray and lone-ly, I just stick___out my chin and grin and say:_____

IT'S THE HARD-KNOCK LIFE

Lyric by Martin Charn
Music by Charles Strou

Annie ™.

WE GOT ANNIE

Lyric by Martin Charnin
Music by Charles Strouse

Spoken: An- nie!

We Got An- nie

We Got An- nie? Yeah!

She's like a shine on your shoes_ or hear-in' a blues_ that's g

Makes you re - lax_ like a big tax_ re - bate.

Spoken: We Got An-nie!

We Got An - nie, We Got

An - nie! And Ben - ny Good - man's got swing,_ Bing is a King_ by

far.

Mutt has got Jeff_ and

El - ean - or F. D. R.

Repeat and Fade

Spoken: We Got An-nie!

I THINK I'M GONNA LIKE IT HERE

Lyric by Martin Cha
Music by Charles Stro

SANDY
(Dumb Dog)

Lyric by Martin Charr...
Music by Charles Strou...

Slowly and Deliberately

LET'S GO TO THE MOVIES

Lyric by Martin Charn
Music by Charles Strou

SIGN!

Lyric by Martin Charn
Music by Charles Strous

36

I DON'T NEED ANYTHING BUT YOU

Lyric by Martin Charnin
Music by Charles Strouse

Annie

YOU'RE NEVER FULLY DRESSED WITHOUT A SMILE

Lyric by Martin Charnin
Music by Charles Strouse

LITTLE GIRLS

Lyric by Martin Charni
Music by Charles Strous

48

EASY STREET

Lyric by Martin Charnin
Music by Charles Strouse

Annie ™.

Annie
T.M.